To Gina —

A faith-filled
fellow journey-er
whose support and love
I deeply treasure
— and always, with my
love — Donna —

Joyeux Noël 2007

The GENTLE ART of a SERVANT'S HEART

CHARLES R. SWINDOLL

COUNTRYMAN

The Gentle Art of a Servant's Heart
Copyright © 1998 by Charles R. Swindoll
Published by J. Countryman®, a division of
Thomas Nelson Inc., Nashville, Tennessee 37214

Managing Editor: Terri Gibbs
Project Editor: Pat Matuszak

Unless otherwise noted, all Scripture is from the New King James
Version. Copyright© 1979, 1980, 1982, Thomas Nelson, Inc.,
Publishers.

Illustrations are from the paintings of Vincent van Gogh (1853-90)

A J. Countryman ® book

Designed by Koechel Peterson, Inc., Minneapolis, Minnesota

Printed in the USA

ISBN: 08499-1501-5

The GENTLE ART of a SERVANT'S HEART

Foreword

In the gallery of His priceless work, the Lord God has included a portrait of vast value. It is the portrait of a servant carefully painted in words that take time to understand and appreciate. The frame in which the portrait has been placed is Jesus Christ's immortal Sermon on the Mount. We return here to see what will help us become the kind of persons the Artist has portrayed. In His word-portrait of a servant, Christ emphasizes eight characteristics or qualities:

Blessed are the poor in spirit, for theirs is the
    kingdom of heaven.
Blessed are those who mourn, for they shall be comforted.
Blessed are the meek, for they shall inherit the earth.
Blessed are those who hunger and thirst for righteousness,
    for they shall be filled.

Blessed are the merciful, for they shall obtain mercy.
Blessed are the pure in heart, for they shall see God.
Blessed are the peacemakers, for they shall be
    called sons of God.
Blessed are those who have been persecuted for
    righteousness' sake, for theirs is the kingdom
    of heaven.

MATTHEW 5:3–11

You don't run through an art gallery; you walk very slowly. You often stop to study the treasured works of art, taking the time to appreciate what has been painted. You examine the texture, the technique, the choice and mixture of colors, the subtle as well as the bold strokes of the brush, the shadings.

As you consider God's portrait of a gentle servant remember—the more valuable the canvas, the more time and thought it deserves.

Blessed are the poor in spirit,

for theirs is the kingdom of heaven.
MATTHEW 5:3

The attitude of being poor in spirit is one of absolute, unvarnished humility. What an excellent way to begin the servant's portrait! It is the portrait of one who sees himself/herself as spiritually bankrupt, deserving of nothing . . . who turns to Almighty God in total trust.

The spirit of humility

is very rare in our day of strong-willed, proud-as-a-

peacock attitudes. Christ Jesus offers genuine, lasting

happiness to those whose hearts willingly declare:

"Oh, Lord
I am a shell full of dust,
animated with an invisible rational soul
and made anew by an unseen power of grace."

—ARTHUR BENNETT, *The Valley of Vision*

Trust in Him at all times, you people;

pour out your heart before Him; God is a refuge for us.
PSALM 62:8

A special promise follows the trait

of spiritual helplessness: ". . . for theirs is the

kingdom of heaven," says Jesus.

Now we see in a mirror, dimly, but
then face to face. Now I know in part,
but then I shall know just as I also am known.

1 CORINTHIANS 13:12

The indispensable condition

of receiving a part in the kingdom of heaven

is acknowledging our spiritual poverty.

For we are His workmanship,

created in Christ Jesus for good works,

which God prepared beforehand

that we should walk in them.

EPHESIANS 2:10

First and foremost in the life of an authentic

servant is a deep, abiding dependency on the living

Lord. On the basis of that attitude, the kingdom of

heaven is promised.

How great is the love the Father has lavished on us,

that we should be called children of God!
1 JOHN 3:1 (NIV)

The person with a servant's heart—not unlike

a child trusting completely in his parent's provision—

is promised a place in Christ's kingdom.

Let the words of my mouth and the
meditation of my heart be acceptable
in Your sight, O LORD, my strength
and my Redeemer.

PSALM 19:14

Jesus was determined to instill in His

disciples character traits of humility and authenticity.

His unique teaching cut through the facade of

religion like a sharp knife through warm butter.

Be kind to one another, tenderhearted,

forgiving one another,

even as God in Christ forgave you.

EPHESIANS 4:32

The Colors of Compassion

PASSION

Blessed are those who mourn,

for they shall be comforted.
MATTHEW 5:4

To mourn is a heavy word—

a passionate lament for one who was loved

with profound devotion. It conveys the sorrow

of a broken heart that includes compassion,

a sincere caring for others.

How happy are those

who care intensely for the hurts and sorrows and

losses of others. At the heart of this character trait

is COMPASSION, another servant attitude so

desperately needed today.

The Savior promises

"...they shall be comforted."

Comfort will be theirs to claim. I find it significant

that no mention is made of the source or the channel.

Simply, it will come. Perhaps from the same one the

servant cared for back when there was a need.

There can be little comfort where there has been no grief.

Do not be anxious about anything, but in everything, by prayer and petition, with thanksgiving, present your requests to God. And the peace of God, which transcends all understanding, will guard your hearts and your minds, in Christ Jesus.

PHILIPPIANS 4:6–7 (NIV)

By this we know love, because He laid down His life for us. And we also ought to lay down our lives for the brethren.

1 JOHN 3:16

A true servant stays in touch with the struggles others experience. There is that humility of mind that continually looks for ways to serve and to give.

God has poured out his love into

our hearts by the Holy Spirit.
ROMANS 5:5 (NIV)

One of the best ways to lead people into a willing spirit is to model it. That involves things like reaching out without being invited and sensing deep hurts without being told. This is a telltale sign of authentic servant-giving. It is impossible to give of ourselves at arm's length. Personal involvement is essential, not incidental.

As you therefore have received Christ Jesus as Lord,

so walk in Him.
COLOSSIANS 2:6

True servants are like their

Lord, compassionate.

He who has begun a good work in you will complete it until the day of Jesus Christ.

PHILIPPIANS 1:6

Blessed are the gentle,

for they shall inherit the earth.
MATTHEW 5:5 (NIV)

Gentleness includes such enviable qualities as

having strength under control—being calm and peaceful

when surrounded by a heated atmosphere.

A gentle servant emits a soothing effect and possesses tact and gracious courtesy that causes others to retain their self-esteem and dignity.

Jesus' gentleness invites:

"Come to Me, all who labor and are heavy laden, and I will give you rest. Take My yoke upon you and learn from Me, for I am gentle and lowly in heart, and YOU WILL FIND REST FOR YOUR SOULS."

MATTHEW 11:28-29

The word for gentleness in Greek

can have several meanings:

- A wild stallion that has been tamed, brought under control
- Carefully chosen words that soothe strong emotions
- Ointment that takes the fever and sting out of a wound
- Tender care like that given by a physician
- Those who are polite and courteous

Clearly, it includes a Christlikeness, since the same word is used to describe His own makeup.

"...for they shall inherit the earth"

can be understood in one of two ways—now or

later. Either "they will ultimately win out in this

life" or "they will be given vast territories in the

kingdom, to judge and to rule." Instead of losing,

the gentle gain—they come out ahead!

Those who wait on the LORD,

they shall inherit the earth.
PSALM 37:9

In the ultimate victory the gentle

will win. Believe that, servant-in-the-making!

Be different from the system!

Imitate those who through faith and

patience inherit what has been promised.
HEBREWS 6:12 (NIV)

Trust your heavenly Father

to keep His promise regarding your inheritance.

It is you who will be blessed.

Clothe yourselves with compassion,

kindness, humility, gentleness and patience.
COLOSSIANS 3:12 (NIV)

Servants with renewed minds

have a perspective on life and power to live life

that is altogether unique—divinely empowered.

That explains how wrongs can be forgiven, and

how offenses can be forgotten.

Do not be conformed to this world, but be transformed by the renewing of your mind, that you may prove what is that good and acceptable and perfect will of God.

ROMANS 12:2

Blessed are those who hunger and thirst for

righteousness, for they shall be filled.

MATTHEW 5:6

The true servant possesses an

insatiable appetite for what is right,

a passionate drive for justice.

The servant who thirsts for righteousness is

engaged in a pursuit of God . . . a hot, restless,

eager longing to walk with Him, to please Him.

> We drink of Thee, the Fountainhead,
> And thirst our souls from Thee to fill.

—BERNARD OF CLARIVEAUX

I will ask the Father, and he will give you
another Counselor to be with you forever —
the Spirit of truth. . . . You know him, for
he lives with you and will be in you.

JOHN 14:16–17 (NIV)

Righteousness includes not just looking

upward, pursuing a vertical holiness, but also

looking around and being grieved over the

corruption, the inequities, the lack of integrity,

the moral compromises that abound.

The servant hungers and thirsts

for right on earth. Unwilling simply to sigh and

shrug off the lack of justice and purity as inevitable.

Be imitators of God, therefore, as dearly loved
children and live a life of love, just as
Christ loved us and gave himself up for us.

EPHESIANS 5:1 (NIV)

Hunger is my native place in the land of the passions: hunger for fellowship, hunger for righteousness—for a fellowship founded on righteousness.

DAG HAMMARSKJOLD

I press toward the goal for the prize of the upward call of God in Christ Jesus

PHILIPPIANS 3:1 4

Servants press on

for righteousness. Some would call them

idealists or dreamers.

> He made Him who knew no sin to be
> sin for us, that we might become the
> righteousness of God in Him.
>
> 2 CORINTHIANS 5:21

What will happen when this passionate appetite is a part of one's life? What does Jesus promise? ". . .they shall be filled."

Jesus said, ". . . whoever drinks the water I give him will never thirst. Indeed, the water I give him will become in him a spring of water welling up to eternal life."

JOHN 4:1 4 (NIV)

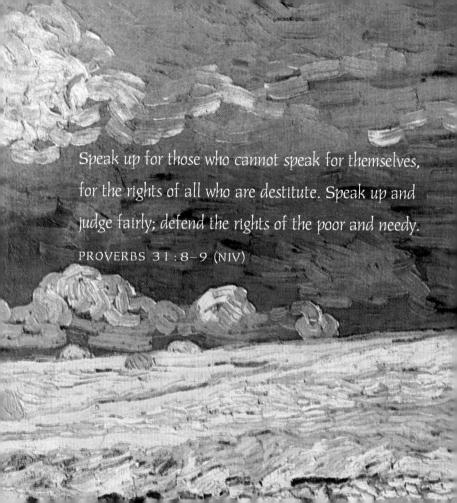

Speak up for those who cannot speak for themselves,
for the rights of all who are destitute. Speak up and
judge fairly; defend the rights of the poor and needy.

PROVERBS 31:8-9 (NIV)

MERCY

The Depth of Mercy

Blessed are the merciful,

for they shall obtain mercy.
MATTHEW 5:7

Mercy is concern for people in need.

It is ministry to the miserable. Offering help

for those who hurt.

Mercy means the ability to get right inside the other person's skin—a deliberate effort of the mind and of the will.

Love one another fervently
with a pure heart.

1 PETER 1:22

Those special servants of God who extend mercy to the miserable often do so with much encouragement because they identify with the sorrowing. Rather than watching from a distance or keeping the needy safely at arm's length, servants of mercy get in touch, involved, and offer assistance that alleviates some of the pain.

If you have a friend who is in need . . . and you say
to him, "Well, good-bye and God bless you; stay
warm and eat hearty," and then don't give him
clothes or food, what good does that do?

JAMES 2:15-16, TLB

True servants are merciful.

They care. They get involved.

They offer more than pious words.

O the bliss of one who identifies with and assists others in need—who gets inside their skin so completely he sees with their eyes and thinks with their thoughts and feels with their feelings. The one who does that will find that others do the same for him when he is in need.

Keep on loving each other.

HEBREWS 13:1 (NIV)

Let us not grow weary while doing good, for in due

season we shall reap if we do not lose heart.
GALATIANS 6:9

And what do they get in return?

What does Christ promise? "...and they shall

obtain mercy"—both from other people as well as

from God Himself.

Jesus, our Savior, came to earth.

By becoming human He got right inside our skin,

literally. That made it possible for Him to see life

through our eyes, feel the sting of our pain, and

identify with the anguish of human need.

Jesus understands.

Jesus the Son of God is our great High Priest who has gone to heaven itself to help us; therefore let us never stop trusting him. This High Priest of ours understands our weaknesses.

HEBREWS 4:14–15, TLB

A Treasure of Purity

Blessed are the pure in heart,

for they shall see God.
MATTHEW 5:8

The quality of purity emphasizes the inner man . . . the motive . . . the "heart."

Purity does not refer simply to doing the right things, but doing the right things *for the right reason*. Being free from *duplicity, hypocrisy, and/or sham*. God desires His servants to be "real" people—authentic to the core. The portrait He paints is realistic.

Christ promises that consistent

servants who are pure in heart "shall see God."

There is no doubt about the destiny of these individuals. For sure, some glorious day in the future, these servants will see the Lord and hear the most significant words that will ever enter human ears: "Well done... enter into the joy of your master." (Matthew 25:21)

The kingdom of heaven is like treasure hidden in a field, which a man found and hid; and for joy over it he goes and sells all that he has and buys that field.

MATTHEW 13:44

Let me challenge you to become "pure in

heart." Think about what it would mean, what

changes you would have to make, what masks you'd

have to peel off.

The Lord is my helper;

I will not fear.
HEBREWS 13:6

Servants who are "pure in heart" have

peeled off their masks. And God places special

blessing on their lives.

Let your speech

always be with grace.
COLOSSIANS 4:6

It is doubtful Jesus despised anything

among those who claimed to serve God more

than hypocrisy— a lack of purity of heart. It

represented the antithesis of servanthood. 🌿

Create in me a clean heart, O God, and
renew a steadfast spirit within me. . . . Restore
to me the joy of Your salvation, and uphold
me by Your generous Spirit.

PSALM 51:10,12

The term pure literally means "clean." It's the idea of being uncontaminated, without corruption or alloy. Without guile . . . sincere and honest in motive.

Man looks at
the outward
appearance,
but the LORD
looks at the heart.

1 SAMUEL 16:7

The Brushstrokes of the Peacemaker

MAKER

Blessed are the peacemakers,

for they shall be called sons of God.
MATTHEW 5:9

This is the only time in all the New Testament that the Greek term translated "peacemakers" appears. It does not mean "Blessed are the passive, those who compromise their convictions." The overall thrust of Scripture is the imperative, "make peace!"

If it is possible, as much as it depends on you,

live peaceably with all men.
ROMANS 12:18

A "peacemaker" is the servant who is at ease with himself—internally, at ease, not agitated, ill-tempered, in turmoil and therefore not abrasive—works hard to settle quarrels, not start them, is accepting, tolerant, finds no pleasure in being negative.

Let us pursue the things which make for peace

and the things by which one may edify another
ROMANS 14:19

Peacemakers watch their tongues and

heal rather than hurt. Solomon gives us this

wise counsel: "A soft answer turns away

wrath" (Proverbs 15:1)

The Lord Jesus states

a marvelous promise that peacemakers can claim:

"...they shall be called sons of God." God's

children. Few things are more godlike than peace.

When we promote it, pursue it, model it, we are

linked directly with Him.

Let the peace of God rule in your hearts, to which

also you were called in one body; and be thankful.
COLOSSIANS 3:15

We don't need more knowledge than

we already have. All we need is the will to

do what needs to be done.

Let us hold unswervingly to the hope we profess, for he who promised is faithful.

HEBREWS 10:23 (NIV)

A Panorama of Patient Experience

Blessed are those who have been persecuted for

righteousness' sake, for theirs is the kingdom of heaven.
MATTHEW 5:10

Realistically, wrong treatment often comes

upon those who do what is right. It's tough to bear!

But the Savior says you will be "blessed" when you

endure it—promising a great reward for your

patient, mature endurance.

We know that all things work together

for good to those who love God.
ROMANS 8:28-29

There are times when the only way

servants can make it through such severe times

without becoming bitter is by focusing on the

ultimate rewards that are promised.

Blessed are you when men revile you, and persecute you, and say all kinds of evil against you falsely, on account of Me. Rejoice and be glad, for your reward in heaven is great, for so they persecuted the prophets who were before you.

MATTHEW 5:11–12 (NIV)

Jesus even says we are to "rejoice and be

glad" as we think on the great rewards He will give

to us in heaven.

Find rest, O my soul, in God alone; my hope comes from him. He alone is my rock and my salvation; he is my fortress, I will not be shaken.

PSALM 62:5-6 (NIV)

Jesus— the One who first painted the servant's portrait—never promised us a rose garden. He came up front with and admitted that the arena of this world is not a friend of grace to help us on to God. Nevertheless He went on to tell all godly servants in every generation that their influence would be nothing short of remarkable.

Jesus said that His servants would be the salt of the earth and they would be the light of the world. So far-reaching would be the influence of servants in society, their presence would be as significant as salt on food and as light on darkness. —Even though it may not admit it, society needs both salt and light.

Neither salt nor light is loud or externally impressive, but both are essential.

May God honor His name as you

and I commit ourselves anew to improving

our serve, to cultivating the art of unselfish

living, serving and giving to others.